THE LITHIUM PACT

Mercosur's Resource Revolution and the Alliance That Could Redefine Global Power

Milton Rothbard

Disclaimer

This book is a work of nonfiction. All historical events, geopolitical analyses, and factual descriptions are accurate to the best of the author's knowledge. Certain scenes, dialogues, characters, and quotations are fictionalized or invented for illustrative purposes. These narrative elements are used solely to clarify historical dynamics and do not represent actual statements or actions by real individuals.

Author's Note

The Lithium Pact is the product of years of studying economics, international trade, geopolitics, defense policy, and global supply chains. The analyses and scenarios presented in this book draw upon information gathered from a wide range of international newspapers, economic publications, public policy discussions, and historical sources from around the world.

While the geopolitical developments described herein are speculative and illustrative, they are grounded in real-world economic principles, strategic considerations, and historical patterns of international cooperation.

The opinions, interpretations, and projections expressed in this work are those of the author and reflect an effort to explore how resources, trade, technology, and alliances may shape the future international order.

TABLE OF CONTENTS

"In all my voyages from Lisbon to the Indies, never have I met men whose word is iron like the Samurai of Japan. Their lords rule with silence, their warriors bow with fire in their eyes, and yet in matters of trade they are as straight as the blade they carry. Among all the peoples of the Orient, there are none more honorable to bargain with than these sons of Bushidō."

— Duarte Álvares, Merchant of the Carreira da Índia, 1603

PROLOGUE — The Age of the Pact

They would later say the world changed quietly, like a tide turning in the dark. No grand speeches. No parades. No thunder of armies crossing borders. Just a whisper that began in the southern hemisphere — a whisper carried by lithium winds, by the hum of refineries in the Atacama, by the deep-earth rumble of a continent awakening.

For decades, Mercosur had been treated as a marketplace, not a power. A region rich enough to tempt empires, yet divided enough to be dismissed by them. But history has a habit of circling back to the places everyone overlooks. And in the early years of the new century, the overlooked began to sharpen their edges.

It started with a question asked behind closed doors in Brasília, Buenos Aires, Asunción, Montevideo:

What if our resources were not our burden — but our leverage?

What if the lithium beneath the salt flats, the rare earths buried under red clay, the grain that fed half the world, the water that would soon be worth more than gold — what if all of it could be forged into something greater than profit?

What if it could become power?

Across the Pacific, two island nations listened. Japan — disciplined, precise, forged by centuries of honor. Taiwan — defiant, innovative, standing unblinking in the shadow of a giant. They had technology. They had industry. They had the will to resist the coming storm.

But they needed something Mercosur had in abundance.

And Mercosur needed something only they could offer.

Not trade.

Not treaties.

A pact.

A pact that would fuse the South American heartland with the Indo-Pacific frontier. A pact that would exchange natural wealth for modern steel, for radar that could see beyond horizons, for alliances that could outlast the century. A pact that would redraw maps without firing a shot.

The world did not see it coming.

But you — the reader — are standing at the edge of it now.

Feel the weight of this moment.

Feel the hum beneath your feet.

Feel the readiness rising in your chest.

Because this is not just the story of resources or diplomacy.

This is the story of nations learning to stand taller.

Of continents discovering their voice.

Of alliances born not from fear, but from purpose.

This is the dawn of The Lithium Pact.

And once you step into this world, nothing will look the same again.

CHAPTER I — The Winds of Freedom

The first signs were not loud. They never are.

Revolutions rarely begin with gunfire; they begin with a change in the air — a shift so subtle that only the attentive feel it. And in the southern half of the world, that shift came as wind.

It swept across the pampas at dawn, bending the tall grass like a field of soldiers bowing in unison. It carried the scent of salt from the Salar de Uyuni, where lithium slept beneath ancient crusts of white. It whispered through the forests of Paraná, rustling leaves older than the nations that claimed them. It rolled over the Paraná River like a drumbeat, steady and patient.

Those who listened closely understood:

Mercosur was waking up.

For generations, the region had been treated as a treasure chest without a guardian — a place where the world came to take, not to partner. Empires had carved it, corporations had mined it, and politicians had bartered it away grain by grain, barrel by barrel, ton by ton.

"But winds do not rise without reason; they rise because the world itself is shifting."

A new generation of leaders — some young, some battle-scarred, all uncomfortably aware of the century ahead — began to ask a question their predecessors had feared:

Why must we remain the world's suppliers, but never its strategists?

In Brasília, a minister stared at a map of the continent and saw not borders, but potential.

In Buenos Aires, an economist traced the lithium triangle with her finger and whispered, "This is our oil."

In Asunción, a general looked at outdated equipment and felt the sting of humiliation.

In Montevideo, a diplomat reread the treaties that had kept the region docile and felt something ancient stir — pride.

The winds carried these thoughts from capital to capital, knitting them together like threads of a long-forgotten tapestry. And as they did, a realization took root:

Freedom is not merely the absence of chains.

Freedom is the ability to choose your alliances.

Across the Pacific, two island nations felt the same winds — though they arrived as typhoons and monsoon rains. Japan, disciplined and deliberate, sensed the tremor of opportunity. Taiwan, resilient and unyielding, recognized the value of partners who understood what it meant to live under the shadow of giants.

They saw Mercosur not as a market, but as a force.

Not as a supplier, but as a pillar.

Not as a distant continent, but as a future ally.

And so the winds of freedom crossed oceans.

They swept through Tokyo's neon canyons, where engineers worked through the night on machines that could see the invisible.

They brushed the shores of Kaohsiung, where shipyards hammered steel into shapes that would define the next century.

They stirred the minds of strategists who understood that the world was entering an age where geography mattered less than resolve.

The winds carried a message — simple, undeniable, electrifying:

The South is rising.

The East is ready.

And together, they can reshape the world.

But winds alone do not change history.

People do.

Decisions do.

Pacts do.

And soon, the first meeting would be called — quiet, discreet, and world-altering.

The winds of freedom had arrived. Yet the winds were not rising in a vacuum. Across the world, the foundations of the old order were beginning to tremble. Supply chains that had once stretched effortlessly across oceans were fracturing under the weight of rivalry and conflict. Wars revealed the fragility of global commerce. Semiconductors became instruments of national power. Rare minerals became strategic assets. Nations that controlled technology sought resources, while nations rich in resources sought security, industry, and influence. The age of complacent globalization was fading, replaced by an era of competition, resilience, and strategic partnerships. For those paying attention, the message was unmistakable: the century ahead would belong not to those who possessed wealth alone, but to those who knew how to transform wealth into power.

Far from the halls of government, Mario Lebron leaned over a table covered with maps, trade statistics, and historical records. His career had been spent studying empires—why some rose, why others declined, and why resource-rich nations so often remained dependent on stronger powers. As his finger traced the lithium triangle stretching across South America, he saw more than minerals beneath the earth. He saw leverage. He saw opportunity. He saw the possibility of a continent finally learning the lesson history had taught for centuries: resources alone create wealth, but resources joined to strategy create power. For the first time in generations, the pieces were beginning to align.

Mario Lebron

Economist, historian, and strategic affairs researcher

"In Buenos Aires I found a city that breathes like a great beast of the South — restless, proud, and forever reaching toward the horizon. Its port is a thunder of ropes, sails, and voices, yet its people carry a warmth that softens even the hardest traveler. I came seeking knowledge of distant lands, but instead I discovered a spirit unbroken by empire and unafraid of tomorrow. If the world has a frontier where courage is born each morning, it is here, upon these windswept shores."

— Kenzo Watanabe, Reflections of a Wandering Scholar, 1825

CHAPTER II — The First Tremors

History does not announce its turning points.

It reveals them in fragments — a conversation overheard, a report dismissed, a meeting postponed, a rumor that refuses to die. And in the months that followed the first winds of freedom, these fragments began to surface across the Southern Cone like tremors before an earthquake.

They appeared first in the numbers.

In Brasília, analysts noticed that lithium exports were rising faster than projected, yet profits were shrinking. Middlemen were multiplying. Foreign firms were tightening their grip. The continent was rich, but the wealth was flowing outward like water through open fingers.

In Buenos Aires, a quiet study circulated among senior ministers. It warned that Argentina's mineral reserves — lithium, copper, rare earths — were becoming "globally indispensable." The report ended with a single line underlined twice:

"Indispensable does not mean powerful — unless we choose to make it so."

In Asunción, a military attaché returned from a conference in Seoul with a troubling observation:

Asian nations were preparing for a century of rivalry. They were arming, fortifying, innovating. And they were searching — urgently — for reliable partners.

In Montevideo, a diplomat received a message from a Japanese counterpart. It was polite, understated, almost ceremonial. But its meaning was unmistakable:

"We believe the future will reward those who build bridges across oceans."

These were the first tremors.

Small.

Quiet.

But unmistakable to those who knew how to listen.

The second tremor came from the markets.

Semiconductor shortages rippled across the globe, halting factories from Detroit to Düsseldorf. Nations that once mocked the idea of "strategic minerals" now scrambled to secure them. Lithium prices surged. Copper became a geopolitical currency. Rare earths were spoken of with the same reverence once reserved for oil.

For the first time in decades, Mercosur was not reacting to the world — the world was reacting to Mercosur.

And in Tokyo, this shift did not go unnoticed.

Japan's Ministry of Economy, Trade and Industry convened a closed-door session. Charts glowed on the walls: supply chains, mineral flows, risk maps. A single conclusion emerged:

"If we do not diversify, we will be vulnerable.

If we do not partner, we will be isolated."

Taiwan reached the same conclusion, but with greater urgency.

Its semiconductor empire — the beating heart of the digital age — depended on minerals it did not control. And the shadow looming across the strait grew longer each year.

The tremors were becoming waves.

But the third tremor — the one that would change everything — did not come from a single leader, a single capital, or a single strategist.

It came from a convergence of needs so powerful that history itself seemed to lean forward.

Japan needed natural resources.

Taiwan needed minerals and energy.

Mercosur needed leverage and technology.

And the world needed stability.

These truths did not emerge in speeches or declarations.

They surfaced quietly — in trade reports, in diplomatic cables, in late-night strategy sessions where maps glowed under dim lights and the future felt dangerously close.

Across continents, a realization began to crystallize:

No nation could navigate the coming century alone.

But together — the South and the East could reshape it.

Outside, the winds of freedom stirred again — stronger, heavier, carrying with them the unmistakable pulse of a new era forming just beyond the horizon.

The Lithium Pact had not yet been born.

But its shadow had begun to fall across the world.

"A nation that stands alone may survive a season, but a nation that chooses its partners wisely can shape a century. In South America we see not a distant continent, but a mirror of our own struggle —

proud peoples guarding resources the world covets, seeking the strength to defend their future. A partnership between Taiwan and the nations of the South is not merely strategic; it is the meeting of two frontiers of resilience. Together, we can turn minerals into security, distance into unity, and uncertainty into power."

— General Chiang Kai-Shek, Vision of Taiwan Doctrine, 1924

CHAPTER III — Soybean, Citrus & Radars in Motion

The first movements of history are rarely military.

They begin in the mundane — in crates, in cargo, in contracts inked at dawn.

And so it was with the early stirrings of the Lithium Pact.

Before diplomats met, before generals exchanged salutes, before any alliance was spoken aloud, the world felt the shift in something deceptively simple:

trade.

Not the old trade — the one dictated by distant capitals and faceless corporations — but a new kind, pulsing with intent.

It began with soybeans.

From the vast plains of Argentina and Brazil, the harvest moved with unusual precision. Ships left port not for their usual destinations, but for new ones — Osaka, Yokohama, Kaohsiung. The manifests were ordinary, but the pattern was not. Someone watching closely would have noticed that the shipments were larger, more frequent, and negotiated with a level of trust normally reserved for long-standing allies.

Japan's agricultural ministry took note.

Taiwan's trade office took interest.

And Mercosur's exporters felt something they had not felt in decades:

leverage.

Soybeans were no longer just food.

They were signals.

Signals that the South could feed the East — and the East was ready to reciprocate.

Then came citrus.

Uruguayan and Paraguayan growers, long overshadowed by global giants, found themselves courted by delegations who spoke not of price, but of partnership. Citrus shipments — oranges, lemons, mandarins — became diplomatic messengers, crossing the Pacific with the quiet dignity of envoys.

In Tokyo, chefs praised the sweetness.

In Taipei, markets sold out within hours.

In Mercosur, farmers realized that their orchards had become instruments of foreign policy.

Citrus was no longer just fruit.

It was soft power.

But the true shift — the one that made the world's strategists sit up — came not from fields or orchards, but from the sky.

Radars.

Japan's defense engineers had been studying Mercosur's geography for months. The vast plains, the open skies, the long coastlines — all ideal for early-warning systems. Taiwan's technicians, masters of compact and resilient design, saw an opportunity to test new generations of sensors far from hostile eyes.

And so, quietly, discreetly, without fanfare or headlines, the first shipments arrived.

Not weapons.

Not missiles.

Not anything that could be called aggressive.

Just radars — the eyes of a modern nation.

They were installed on hillsides overlooking the Atlantic, on plateaus where the wind never stopped, on ridges where condors circled. Local crews worked side by side with Japanese and Taiwanese specialists, sharing tools, sharing knowledge, sharing purpose.

For the first time in its history, Mercosur could see farther than its borders.

And for the first time, Japan and Taiwan had partners who understood that security was not a gift — it was a pact.

Soybeans fed trust.

Citrus sweetened diplomacy.

Radars forged resolve.

Three currents, moving in parallel, converging into something larger than any of them alone.

Across the world, analysts noticed.

Some dismissed it as coincidence.

Others saw the pattern forming.

A few who understood how empires rise — felt a chill.

Because these were not random transactions.

They were the first motions of a new alignment.

A South-to-East axis.

A partnership of necessity and vision.

A quiet revolution carried not by armies, but by agriculture and antennas.

The Lithium Pact was still unspoken.

Still unofficial.

Still forming in the shadows.

But its momentum was undeniable.

And soon, the world would no longer be able to ignore.

"Give me a place to stand, and I will move the world."

— Archimedes

CHAPTER IV — Taigei-Class Submarine & The Lithium Technology

The world's great alliances are rarely born in conference halls.

They begin in shipyards, in factories, in the quiet hum of machines that shape the future long before diplomats give it a name.

And so it was with the next movement of the Lithium Pact.

Not a treaty.

Not a declaration.

But an exchange — raw power for refined mastery.

It began in the Pacific, beneath the waves.

Japan's Taigei-class submarine — sleek, silent, a creature of steel and shadow — represented the pinnacle of modern naval engineering. Its hull was shaped by centuries of maritime discipline. Its systems were forged in the crucible of an island nation that had learned, through war and peace alike, that survival depended on seeing danger before it surfaced.

But beneath its quiet exterior lay something new.

A heart powered not by diesel alone, nor by nuclear fire, but by advanced lithium-ion technology — batteries capable of holding vast reserves of energy, allowing the vessel to glide through the deep with a silence that borders on myth.

Japan had mastered the art of turning lithium into stealth.

South America had mastered the art of pulling lithium from the earth.

The symmetry was impossible to ignore.

In Buenos Aires, a delegation studied the Taigei's schematics with a mixture of awe and calculation. They saw not a weapon, but a symbol — proof that their minerals could become more than exports. They could become engines of sovereignty.

In Brasília, engineers traced the supply chain of the submarine's battery modules. Every line led back to the same truth:

"We have the raw materials.

They have the refinement.

Together, we have power."

In Santiago, Chilean officials — guardians of the world's largest lithium reserves — recognized the opportunity. For decades, they had sold lithium as dust, as ore, as the first step in someone else's wealth. Now, for the first time, they saw a path to sell lithium as destiny.

The exchange began quietly.

Argentina offered lithium carbonate at stable, long-term rates — not as a commodity, but as a strategic asset.

Brazil offered niobium, rare earths, and industrial capacity — the metals that strengthen steel and shape the skeletons of machines.

Chile offered purity — the highest-grade lithium on Earth, drawn from salt flats older than civilization.

Japan responded not with cash, but with technology:

battery refinement systems

submarine-grade energy modules

robotics for mineral extraction

precision manufacturing lines

training programs for South American engineers

and the crown jewel — early access to Taigei-class battery architecture

It was not charity.

It was not dependency.

It was equilibrium.

A fair trade between continents that had long been told they must accept the world as it is.

Now, they were shaping the world as it could be.

In a shipyard in Kobe, a Taigei-class submarine slid into the water under a moonlit sky. Its lithium heart pulsed with energy drawn from minerals that had slept for millennia beneath the South American desert.

In a factory in São Paulo, Japanese technicians trained Brazilian workers to assemble battery modules once considered too advanced to export.

In a laboratory in Santiago, Chilean chemists refined lithium hydroxide to a purity level that stunned their Japanese counterparts.

In a naval base in Mar del Plata, Argentine officers studied the doctrine of silent deterrence — the art of defending a coastline not with noise, but with presence.

Across the hemisphere, a new understanding took root:

Raw materials are wealth.

Technology is power.

But together, they are independence.

The world watched — some with curiosity, others with unease.

Because this was no longer just soybeans, citrus, or radars.

This was the merging of earth and steel, minerals and machines, South and East.

This was the moment the Lithium Pact stopped whispering and began to speak.

And soon, the world would have no choice but to listen.

"The ninja moves through darkness as the moon moves through clouds — unseen, unheard, yet altering the fate of all below. To face such a warrior is to fear a shadow; to command such a warrior is to hold the power of silence itself. In every age, the strongest blade is not the one that shines, but the one that cannot be found."

— Yamamoto Mishiba, Samurai of the Silent Path, 1752.

CHAPTER V — Understanding Logistics & Equal Fair Trade

Great alliances are not built on ideals alone.

They are built on movement — of ships, of goods, of energy, of trust.

And in the early days of the Lithium Pact, the most important movement was not military or diplomatic, but logistical.

For the first time in decades, South America and Japan were aligning their supply chains, their trade routes, and their economic destinies.

It began with two leaders standing at opposite ends of the Pacific, yet staring at the same horizon.

Buenos Aires — The Return of Economic Breath

Argentina had spent years gasping under the weight of inflation, stagnation, and decay. But under President Javier Milei, something unexpected began to happen — not overnight, not magically, but undeniably.

Ports that had once been symbols of decline began to hum again.

Export terminals moved soy, beef, lithium, and citrus with renewed discipline.

Regulations that strangled industry were cut away like old ropes from a mast.

Foreign investors, long absent, returned cautiously — then eagerly.

Trade offices in Tokyo and Osaka reported a surge of Argentine delegations seeking not loans, but partnerships.

For the first time in a generation, Argentina was not asking the world for relief.

It was offering the world value.

And Japan noticed.

Tokyo — The Rise of a New Era

Japan, too, was entering a moment of transformation.

Under Prime Minister Sanae Takaichi, the nation rediscovered something it had not felt in decades:

pride in its future.

Her administration championed technological sovereignty, industrial revival, and a foreign policy rooted in clarity rather than hesitation. She spoke of alliances not as obligations, but as opportunities — bridges to a world where Japan could stand tall again.

Her message resonated across the Pacific.

In Buenos Aires, Argentine officials admired her decisiveness.

In Tokyo, Japanese ministers admired Argentina's hunger for renewal.

Two nations — one rebuilding its economy, the other revitalizing its identity — found in each other a reflection of their own aspirations.

Admiration became respect.

Respect became alignment.

Alignment became strategy.

The Logistics Revolution

The first joint task force between Argentina and Japan did not discuss ideology.

It discussed ports.

How to modernize the Port of Buenos Aires

How to expand Rosario's export capacity

How to integrate Japanese shipping standards into South American terminals

How to create a Pacific-Atlantic corridor linking Chilean ports to Japanese markets

How to build cold-chain logistics for citrus and beef

How to secure lithium shipments with blockchain-based tracking

This was not glamorous work.

But it was the work that changes nations.

Japan brought precision, discipline, and world-class engineering.

Argentina brought resources, geography, and a willingness to reform.

Together, they began to build a logistical architecture that could withstand the storms of the century ahead.

Equal Fair Trade — The New Doctrine

For decades, South America had exported raw materials and imported finished goods — a cycle that enriched others while weakening itself.

But the Lithium Pact introduced a new principle:

"Equal value for equal value."

Lithium for robotics.

Grain for microchips.

Copper for energy systems.

Beef for industrial machinery.

Rare earths for advanced batteries.

No more asymmetry.

No more dependency.

No more accepting the world as it was.

This was fair trade, not in rhetoric but in practice.

And it was working.

Buenos Aires & Tokyo — A New Axis of Trust

Diplomats from both nations began to speak of each other with unusual warmth.

Argentine envoys admired Japan's discipline, its reliability, its refusal to exploit.

Japanese envoys admired Argentina's courage, its reforms, its hunger to rise.

Meetings that once lasted an hour now lasted three.

Negotiations that once stalled now accelerated.

Projects that once seemed impossible now felt inevitable.

A new axis was forming — not of ideology, not of military force, but of mutual respect.

Buenos Aires and Tokyo were no longer distant capitals.

They were partners in a shared future.

The World Takes Notice

Analysts in Washington, Beijing, and Brussels began to whisper:

"Something is happening between Japan and South America."

They saw:

trade routes shifting

supply chains realigning

logistics modernizing

economies stabilizing

leaders rising

And beneath it all, they sensed the quiet emergence of a new doctrine:

Fair trade is power.

Logistics are sovereignty.

Partnerships are destiny.

The Lithium Pact was no longer a whisper.

It was becoming a structure — one container ship, one port, one agreement at a time.

And soon, the world would feel its weight.

"Commerce is the quiet architect of empires. Armies may seize a moment, but only fair exchange can shape an age. When two distant nations trade with honor, they do more than move goods — they move the destiny of their peoples."

— Marquis Étienne de Rochefort, Reflections on the Order of Nations, 1543

CHAPTER VI — On the Nature of Exchange

History is often told through battles and treaties, but the true engines of civilization are quieter. They move in caravans, in ships, in ledgers inked at dusk. They move in the hands of merchants, engineers, farmers, and sailors — the anonymous millions who carry nations on their backs.

And so, before the Lithium Pact could become strategy, it had to become movement.

Not the movement of armies, but the movement of value.

I. The Invisible Architecture

Every nation stands upon an invisible architecture — a web of ports, roads, warehouses, refineries, and trade routes. Most citizens never see it. Most leaders barely understand it. Yet it is this hidden skeleton that determines whether a country rises or falls.

A nation with resources but no logistics is a giant with broken legs.

A nation with technology but no partners is a lighthouse without a shore.

A nation with ambition but no exchange is a voice lost in the wind.

The Lithium Pact sought to correct these imbalances — not with force, but with equilibrium.

II. The Philosophy of Fair Trade

Fair trade is not charity.

Fair trade is not generosity.

Fair trade is justice measured in tonnage and time.

It is the recognition that:

raw materials hold potential

finished goods hold refinement

logistics hold power

and exchange holds destiny

For centuries, South America exported the first and imported the second.

For decades, Japan refined the second but lacked the first.

The Pact did not invent fairness.

It simply acknowledged it.

III. The Moral Weight of Logistics

To understand logistics is to understand humility.

A ship delayed by a storm can alter the fate of a factory.

A missing component can silence an entire industry.

A port strike can ripple across oceans like a stone thrown into still water.

Nations rise not because they are strong, but because they are coordinated.

The Lithium Pact was not merely an alliance of governments — it was an alliance of systems:

Argentine grain routes

Chilean lithium corridors

Brazilian industrial arteries

Japanese shipping lanes

Taiwanese semiconductor flows

Each one a vein.

Each one a lifeline.

Each one a promise.

IV. The Ethics of Exchange

True exchange requires three virtues:

Respect — the recognition of another nation's dignity.

Transparency — the clarity that prevents exploitation.

Reciprocity — the balance that sustains trust.

Buenos Aires and Tokyo discovered these virtues not in speeches, but in practice.

A shipment delivered on time.

A contract honored without renegotiation.

A delegation welcomed with sincerity.

A technology shared without condescension.

These small acts, repeated across oceans, became the moral foundation of the Pact.

V. The Stillness Before the Next Step

Every great transformation contains a moment of stillness — a pause where the world seems to inhale before exhaling a new reality.

This chapter is that breath.

A moment to understand that the Lithium Pact is not merely a geopolitical maneuver, but a philosophical statement:

Nations do not rise by taking.

They rise by exchanging.

And in that exchange, they discover not only power, but purpose.

The next chapters will return to movement — to ships, to radars, to diplomacy, to strategy.

But here, in this quiet interlude, the reader sees the truth beneath the machinery:

The Pact is not built on lithium.

It is built on understanding.

And understanding is the rarest resource of all.

"I found more honesty in a single Irish handshake than in a dozen English contracts. Trade is cleanest when it flows between those who share hardship, not hierarchy. Scotland and Ireland barter as equals, for neither of us ever cared much for the crown that claimed to rule us both."

— Alastair McDougal, Letters from the Western Sea, 1817

CHAPTER VII — The Blessing and Support of the United States of America

Great alliances do not rise in isolation.

Even the strongest partnerships need a guardian wind — a stabilizing presence that ensures the seas remain navigable and the world remains open to possibility.

For the Lithium Pact, that wind came from the United States of America.

Not as a commander.

Not as an empire.

But as a strategic supporter who understood that a stable South America and a strong Japan were pillars of a balanced century.

I. Washington Takes Notice

The first reports arrived quietly.

Analysts in the Pentagon, the State Department, and the National Security Council began to notice unusual patterns:

Argentine exports rising with discipline

Japanese investment flowing into South American logistics

Chilean lithium refining reaching new levels of purity

Brazilian industrial corridors aligning with Indo-Pacific supply chains

None of these movements were threatening.

All of them were stabilizing.

For the United States, this was not a challenge — it was an opportunity.

A stronger Mercosur meant a more resilient Western Hemisphere.

A revitalized Japan meant a more balanced Indo-Pacific.

A fair-trade alliance meant fewer crises, fewer dependencies, fewer shocks.

Washington understood the deeper truth:

A world with strong partners is safer than a world with desperate ones.

II. The American Doctrine of Support

The United States did not seek to control the Lithium Pact.

It sought to reinforce it.

American strategists saw three benefits:

Stability — A prosperous South America reduces global volatility.

Security — A strong Japan contributes to Indo-Pacific balance.

Supply Chains — Fair trade reduces the fragility of global markets.

Thus emerged a quiet doctrine:

"Support without interference. Encourage without dictating. Strengthen without overshadowing."

It was a rare moment in geopolitics — a great power choosing partnership over dominance.

III. Buenos Aires & Washington — A New Understanding

Argentina's economic recovery had not gone unnoticed.

American economists admired the reforms.

American investors saw opportunity.

American diplomats saw a nation rising with purpose.

Meetings between Buenos Aires and Washington grew warmer, more candid, more aligned.

The United States recognized Argentina not as a client state, but as a strategic partner in a hemisphere that needed stability.

In return, Argentina saw the United States not as a distant superpower, but as a reliable ally whose support could amplify the Pact's reach.

IV. Tokyo & Washington — Old Allies, New Momentum

Japan and the United States had been allies for generations, but the rise of the Lithium Pact gave their partnership new meaning.

American naval officers admired Japan's Taigei-class innovations.

American engineers collaborated on battery research.

American diplomats praised Japan's leadership in fair-trade diplomacy.

The United States understood that Japan's renewed pride and direction were not threats — they were anchors in a turbulent century.

And Japan understood that American support was not conditional — it was foundational.

V. The Blessing

The moment came quietly, without ceremony.

A senior American official, speaking at a closed-door forum, said words that would later be repeated across embassies and ministries:

"A stable South America and a strong Japan are in the interest of the free world.

We support the Lithium Pact."

It was not a treaty.

It was not a declaration.

It was something more powerful:

Legitimacy.

With those words, the Pact gained a shield — not of steel, but of recognition.

The world took notice.

VI. The Triangular Balance

With the United States offering support, a new geometry emerged:

South America — resources, logistics, renewal

Japan — technology, discipline, strategic clarity

United States — stability, security, global reach

Three continents, three strengths, one alignment.

Not an empire.

Not a block.

But a balance.

A balance that promised a century shaped not by domination, but by cooperation.

VII. The World Reacts

Some nations welcomed the development.

Others watched with caution.

A few felt the ground shift beneath their feet.

Because the Lithium Pact was no longer a regional curiosity.

It was becoming a pillar of the emerging world order.

And with the blessing of the United States, its momentum became unstoppable.

The winds of freedom had crossed oceans.

The tremors had become waves.

The motions had become machinery.

The exchanges had become doctrine.

Now, with American support, the Pact had become global.

And the century ahead would feel its weight.

"The nations that will command the future are not those with the largest armies, but those that master the quiet mathematics of exchange. When resources flow with fairness and technology moves with purpose, alliances become stronger than empires — and more enduring than borders."

— Dr. Leopold Hartmann, Lecture on the Economics of Tomorrow, Vienna School of Trade, 1954

CHAPTER VIII — The Symbolism Behind the Tea Ceremony and the Argentine Mate

Nations speak through treaties, but they reveal themselves through rituals.

And among all the rituals of the world, few carry as much quiet power as the Japanese tea ceremony and the Argentine mate.

Two beverages.

Two continents.

Two histories.

Yet one shared truth:

Both are acts of communion.

I. The Japanese Tea Ceremony — Harmony in Stillness

In Japan, tea is not merely prepared.

It is summoned.

The tea ceremony — chanoyu — is a choreography of intention:

the cleansing of the bowl

the measured whisking of matcha

the bow of respect

the silence between gestures

Every movement is deliberate.

Every sound is meaningful.

Every breath is part of the ritual.

The tea ceremony teaches:

wa — harmony

kei — respect

sei — purity

jaku — tranquility

It is a moment where the world slows, where hierarchy dissolves, where host and guest become equals in the presence of a simple bowl of tea.

II. The Argentine Mate — Brotherhood in Motion

On the plains of Argentina, mate is not prepared in silence.

It is prepared in company.

The gourd is filled.

The yerba is shaken.

The water is poured.

And then — the circle begins.

Mate is passed from hand to hand, person to person, story to story.

It is not a drink.

It is a bond.

The ritual teaches:

sharing — one gourd, many hands

trust — the circle is sacred

equality — all drink from the same vessel

presence — conversation is the true beverage

Where tea creates stillness, mate creates connection.

Where tea invites reflection, mate invites dialogue.

Yet both rituals lead to the same destination:

Human unity.

III. What These Two Beverages Have in Common

Though born oceans apart, the tea ceremony and mate share a profound symbolic core:

1. Both are rituals of equality

In tea, the host lowers themselves to serve.

In mate, all drink from the same gourd.

Hierarchy dissolves.

Community rises.

2. Both transform a simple drink into a cultural philosophy

Tea becomes harmony.

Mate becomes brotherhood.

3. Both require patience and presence

You cannot rush tea.

You cannot rush mate.

The ritual is the meaning.

4. Both are gateways to national identity

To understand Japan, watch a tea ceremony.

To understand Argentina, share a mate.

5. Both create bonds stronger than words

Tea binds host and guest.

Mate binds friends and strangers.

In both rituals, the beverage is secondary.

The connection is primary.

IV. The Symbolism for the Lithium Pact

When Japanese diplomats visited Buenos Aires, they were offered mate.

When Argentine envoys visited Tokyo, they were invited to tea.

Two rituals.

Two philosophies.

One message:

"We see you.

We respect you.

We share with you."

The tea ceremony taught Argentina the beauty of stillness.

Mate taught Japan the warmth of shared circles.

Together, they formed a cultural bridge stronger than any treaty.

Because alliances built on strategy endure for years.

Alliances built on understanding endure for generations.

V. The Quiet Power of Ritual

In a world of steel, lithium, submarines, and logistics, it is easy to forget that nations are not machines.

They are people.

And people bond not through contracts, but through rituals — the small, sacred acts that reveal who they are.

Tea and mate are more than beverages.

They are symbols.

Symbols of harmony.

Symbols of equality.

Symbols of shared destiny.

And in the story of the Lithium Pact, they are reminders that the greatest alliances begin not with signatures, but with cups.

"In Tokyo I learned that tea is not merely poured, but revealed. Each gesture is a poem, each silence a philosophy. Among the Japanese, I discovered a truth my own countrymen often forget: a nation's strength is measured not only by its battles, but by the grace of its rituals."

— Lord Charlton McDougal, Journals of an Eastern Voyage, 1749

CHAPTER IX — The Unofficial Meeting in Buenos Aires: Kobe Beef on the Argentine Parrilla

Some alliances are forged in conference rooms.

Others in war rooms.

But the rarest — and strongest — are forged around fire.

The unofficial meeting between the Japanese delegation and the Argentine leadership did not take place in a palace or a ministry.

It took place in a quiet corner of Buenos Aires, in a private courtyard where the scent of burning quebracho wood drifted into the night.

There was no press.

No protocol.

No speeches.

Only a parrilla glowing red, a handful of trusted figures, and a cut of Kobe beef that had traveled across the Pacific like a diplomatic envoy of its own.

I. The Setting — A Night Without Titles

The courtyard belonged to an old friend of the Argentine foreign minister, a man whose name never appeared in newspapers but whose grill was whispered about in diplomatic circles.

The Japanese delegation arrived without fanfare.

No motorcade.

No cameras.

Just quiet footsteps on cobblestone.

The Argentines greeted them not with handshakes, but with embraces — the kind that say, Tonight, we are not officials. We are people.

A single long wooden table stood beneath a string of warm lights.

The parrilla crackled nearby, its iron grates glowing like the bars of a small sun.

II. The Ritual of Fire

The grill master — a man with forearms like carved oak and a face weathered by decades of smoke — approached the Kobe beef with reverence.

He did not season it.

He did not marinate it.

He did not touch it more than necessary.

He simply placed it on the grill and let the fire speak.

The Japanese delegation watched with fascination.

In their culture, Kobe beef was a treasure — prepared with precision, technique, and ceremony.

But here, in Buenos Aires, the ceremony was different:

fire instead of steel

smoke instead of silence

instinct instead of measurement

And yet, the respect was the same.

One of the Japanese envoys whispered:

"In Japan, we honor the cow.

Here, you honor the fire."

The grill master smiled.

"Fire is our tea ceremony."

III. The Conversation — Soft Voices, Hard Truths

As the meat cooked, the conversation flowed.

Not about treaties.

Not about logistics.

Not about lithium or submarines or trade corridors.

But about:

family

childhood

the meaning of work

the pride of craft

the weight of responsibility

the loneliness of leadership

The Japanese spoke of the discipline of their ancestors.

The Argentines spoke of the resilience of their people.

And slowly, the distance between them dissolved.

Because nations may differ — but humans do not.

IV. The Meal — A Fusion of Worlds

When the Kobe beef was finally served, it was placed on a wooden board, sliced with the precision of a surgeon and the humility of a farmer.

The Japanese delegation tasted it first.

Silence.

Then a bow — deep, sincere, grateful.

"This is not Kobe beef anymore," one envoy said softly.

"It is something new."

The Argentines raised their glasses.

"To what we create together."

Wine flowed.

Laughter rose.

Stories crossed oceans.

And in that courtyard, under the warm lights and the scent of woodsmoke, the Lithium Pact gained something no treaty could provide:

Friendship.

V. The Symbolism — Fire Meets Precision

The Kobe beef on the Argentine parrilla became a metaphor whispered later in diplomatic halls:

Japanese excellence

Argentine passion

Shared respect

Mutual trust

A fusion stronger than either alone

It symbolized a truth both nations understood:

Great alliances are not built by signatures.

They are built by shared tables.

VI. The Departure — A Quiet Promise

When the night ended, there were no photographs.

No official statements.

No commemorative plaques.

Only a final exchange of words:

"Our nations will walk together."

"And when the world asks why, we will say:

Because we broke bread — and shared fire."

The Japanese delegation left the courtyard with full stomachs and fuller hearts.

The Argentines watched them go, knowing something profound had happened.

Not a negotiation.

Not a deal.

But a bond.

A bond forged in smoke, salt, and sincerity.

"Food is the first language humans ever spoke. Long before treaties or flags, we learned to trust one another by sharing what we had cooked with our own hands. A meal taken together is not nourishment — it is a pact."

— Jean-Antoine Brillat-Savarin, Reflections for a New Century, 1903

CHAPTER X — The Economy of the Free People

Freedom is not an abstract ideal.

It is an economic structure — a way for nations to exchange value without coercion, dependency, or hidden hierarchies.

As the Lithium Pact matured, its greatest achievement was the creation of a new economic model: the Economy of the Free People.

It did not resemble the old systems of the 20th century.

It was voluntary, balanced, and built on dignity.

I. Leaving the Old Order Behind

For generations, global markets had been shaped by imbalance:

resources extracted without fairness

industries dependent on distant powers

value chains designed to benefit only a few

South America supplied.

Japan refined.

Others dictated.

The Pact broke this pattern by introducing a simple principle:

Prosperity must be mutual, or it is not prosperity at all.

This was not moralism.

It was strategic clarity.

II. The Three Foundations of the New Model

The Economy of the Free People rested on three foundations — practical, measurable, transformative.

1. Balanced Exchange

Every transaction had to benefit both sides.

Lithium for robotics.

Grain for microchips.

Copper for energy systems.

Beef for industrial machinery.

Value flowed in both directions, creating stability instead of dependency.

2. Sovereignty Through Logistics

A nation that cannot move its goods is vulnerable.

The Pact invested heavily in:

deep-water ports

transcontinental rail

cold-chain networks

shipping lanes

energy corridors

digital tracking systems

Logistics became the backbone of independence.

3. Innovation Through Partnership

Technology was no longer guarded behind walls.

Japan contributed precision engineering.

South America contributed resources and scale.

Together they built industries neither could achieve alone.

This was cooperation, not subordination.

III. The Rise of a Market Among Equals

Markets become truly free only when participants negotiate from equal footing.

The Pact created that environment:

Argentina priced its exports based on value, not desperation

Japan invested with transparency, not leverage

Brazil, Chile, Paraguay, and Uruguay joined with confidence, not caution

For the first time, South America was not a supplier in someone else's system.

It was a co-architect of a new one.

IV. The Human Dividend

Economic freedom is measured not in charts, but in lives.

Farmers in Corrientes saw their citrus reach Asia at fair prices.

Engineers in Osaka worked with lithium refined under transparent contracts.

Dockworkers in Montevideo loaded ships with pride.

Technicians in Kobe collaborated with Chilean miners on safety innovations.

The Pact did not enrich elites.

It elevated workers, producers, and craftsmen — the people who carry nations on their shoulders.

V. The American Perspective

Washington observed the transformation with interest.

A stable South America.

A technologically confident Japan.

A fair-trade alliance that reduced global volatility.

American economists described it as:

"The first economic model designed for a multipolar century."

It was not a challenge to the United States.

It was a stabilizing force.

VI. The Philosophy Beneath the Numbers

The Economy of the Free People was not built on ideology.

It was built on principles that could be seen in every transaction:

dignity in production

fairness in exchange

transparency in logistics

respect in negotiation

sovereignty in development

These principles were not slogans.

They were practices.

A shipment delivered on time.

A contract honored without revision.

A technology shared without condescension.

A price negotiated without pressure.

This was economics as integrity.

VII. A Model for the World

Other regions took notice.

Europe studied it.

Africa admired it.

Southeast Asia began to emulate it.

The Pact demonstrated that cooperation could outperform coercion, and that nations could rise together without sacrificing autonomy.

It was a quiet revolution — but revolutions built on fairness rarely need noise.

VIII. The New Architecture

The Economy of the Free People grew steadily, like a structure built from the ground up:

strong foundations

balanced pillars

transparent walls

open doors

It was not designed to dominate.

It was designed to endure.

And as it expanded, it reshaped the global landscape — proving that freedom and prosperity are not rivals, but partners.

The free people had built their economy.

And the century was beginning to bend toward their design.

"¡Viva la libertad, carajo!" — Presidente Javier Milei

"Long live freedom, damn it!" — President Javier Milei

CHAPTER XI — The Strategic Mutual Defense Alliance

(Japan – United States – Taiwan & Mercosur)

Security is the final language of sovereignty.

Economics builds prosperity, but defense preserves it.

And as the Lithium Pact matured, the nations involved understood a truth older than empires:

Prosperity without protection is an invitation to predation.

Thus emerged the most consequential development of the new century —

a Strategic Mutual Defense Alliance linking:

Japan — precision, discipline, maritime reach

The United States — global logistics, deterrence, strategic depth

Taiwan — technological mastery, resilience, semiconductor supremacy

Mercosur — resources, geography, industrial renewal, southern logistics

Four pillars.

Four strengths.

One shield.

I. The Quiet Birth of a New Security Architecture

The alliance did not begin with treaties or declarations.

It began with patterns:

joint naval exercises in the South Atlantic

cyber-security cooperation between Tokyo and Buenos Aires

American logistical support for South American ports

Taiwanese investment in secure communications infrastructure

Japanese training exchanges with Argentine and Brazilian officers

These were not isolated events.

They were the early threads of a strategic tapestry.

Washington saw stability.

Tokyo saw opportunity.

Taipei saw survival.

Mercosur saw sovereignty.

Each nation brought something essential.

Each nation gained something indispensable.

II. The Four Strategic Imperatives

The alliance rested on four imperatives — clear, pragmatic, and mutually reinforcing.

1. Protect the Supply Chains of the Free World

Lithium, semiconductors, rare earths, energy systems —

the arteries of the modern economy.

Japan and Taiwan needed secure access.

Mercosur needed secure export routes.

The United States needed global stability.

Together, they formed a supply-chain shield.

2. Secure the Maritime Corridors

Three oceans mattered:

the Pacific, where Japan and Taiwan faced constant pressure

the Atlantic, where Mercosur's ports fed the world

the Caribbean, the hinge between hemispheres

Joint patrols, shared intelligence, and coordinated logistics created a maritime triangle of stability.

3. Build Interoperable Defense Systems

This was not an arms race.

It was a compatibility race.

shared communication protocols

standardized emergency procedures

joint cyber-defense frameworks

coordinated satellite monitoring

Four nations, one operational language.

4. Deter Aggression Without Provocation

The alliance was not designed to threaten.

It was designed to prevent threats from materializing.

Strength as reassurance.

Unity as deterrence.

Cooperation as stability.

III. The American Role — Stability Without Dominance

The United States did not seek to command the alliance.

It sought to anchor it.

American strategists understood that a world of strong partners was safer than a world of fragile dependencies.

Their contribution was threefold:

logistical depth — global bases, transport fleets, satellite networks

strategic deterrence — the credibility of a major power

interoperability leadership — ensuring all partners could act as one

It was support, not control.

Coordination, not hierarchy.

IV. Japan's Role — Precision and Maritime Mastery

Japan brought discipline, technology, and a navy built for contested waters.

Its contributions included:

advanced anti-submarine warfare

maritime surveillance systems

robotics for logistics and defense

strategic doctrine refined over decades

Japan became the eastern anchor of the alliance.

V. Taiwan's Role — The Technological Heart

Taiwan contributed what no other nation could:

semiconductor supremacy

cyber-defense expertise

resilient infrastructure

asymmetric defense innovation

Its role was not symbolic, it was central.

Protect Taiwan, and you protect the digital nervous system of the modern world.

VI. Mercosur's Role — The Southern Shield

Mercosur brought geography, resources, and industrial potential.

Argentina, Brazil, Chile, Paraguay, and Uruguay contributed:

deep-water ports

southern logistics corridors

rare minerals

agricultural stability

growing aerospace and naval industries

The South Atlantic became the alliance's quiet fortress —

far from the world's flashpoints, yet essential to its balance.

VII. The Pact of Four Winds

Diplomats later called it the Pact of Four Winds:

North Wind — the United States, carrying global reach

East Wind — Japan and Taiwan, guardians of the Pacific

South Wind — Mercosur, the rising hemisphere

West Wind — the shared commitment to freedom and stability

Four winds, one climate:

a world where free nations protect one another.

VIII. The Doctrine of Shared Security

The alliance adopted a simple doctrine:

"If one is threatened, all are diminished.

If one stands firm, all stand stronger."

a promise that prosperity would not be left undefended.

IX. The World Reacts

Some nations welcomed the stability.

Others watched with caution.

A few felt the strategic map shifting beneath their feet.

Because this alliance was not merely defensive.

It was transformational.

It signaled the rise of a new geopolitical geometry —

one not built on domination, but on mutual protection.

X. The Shield of the Free People

The Strategic Mutual Defense Alliance became the final pillar of the Lithium Pact's architecture.

Economics gave it purpose.

Culture gave it soul.

Defense gave it permanence.

And together, these nations forged something rare:

A shield carried not by one nation,

but by many —

for the sake of all who choose freedom.

"Distance weakens only the ties born of convenience.

But the bonds forged for a just purpose endure across oceans and centuries.

For when souls unite in righteousness, no horizon can divide them."

— Brother Aurelius de Tagaste, Monastery of Saint Pelagius, 1600

CHAPTER XII — The Shadow Opposition

Tension, Drama, Global Reaction

Every alliance casts a shadow.

And the stronger the alliance, the longer the shadow becomes.

The Strategic Mutual Defense Alliance — Japan, the United States, Taiwan, and Mercosur — did not rise unnoticed.

It shifted balances, threatened old arrangements, and awakened forces that preferred the world as it had been: predictable, hierarchical, and easy to manipulate.

The opposition did not announce itself.

It whispered.

It probed.

It tested the edges of the new order.

Because power rarely confronts directly.

It moves in the dark.

I. The First Ripples — A World Uneasy

The global reaction was immediate, though not uniform.

Some nations welcomed the stability.

Others feared the precedent.

A few saw their influence shrinking like a tide pulling back from the shore.

Three regions reacted most sharply:

A Eurasian power bloc that relied on fragmented South America

A rising Asian hegemon wary of Japan–Taiwan unity

A consortium of energy states threatened by lithium's ascent

None declared hostility.

All began to maneuver.

The world had entered a new phase:

competition without open conflict.

II. The Tools of the Shadow Opposition

The opposition did not use armies.

It used subtler weapons — the tools of the 21st century.

1. Disinformation Campaigns

Anonymous accounts flooded social networks with narratives designed to fracture trust:

"Mercosur is being exploited."

"Japan is re-militarizing."

"The U.S. is pulling the strings."

"Taiwan is dragging the world into conflict."

None of it was true.

All of it was effective.

2. Cyber Intrusions

Not attacks — tests, probing ports in Montevideo, scanning Japanese satellite networks, and mapping Taiwanese semiconductor infrastructure

attempting to breach U.S. logistics systems

The message was clear:

"We are watching."

3. Economic Pressure

Certain nations quietly:

restricted rare earth exports

manipulated shipping insurance rates

delayed port clearances

offered predatory loans to South American states

The goal was not collapse.

It was doubt.

4. Diplomatic Wedges

Envoys whispered in private rooms:

"Why tie your future to distant nations?"

"Why trust partners who cannot protect you?"

"Why join an alliance that may provoke conflict?"

The opposition understood something ancient:

alliances die from within, not from without.

III. The First Crisis — The Atlantic Interference

The turning point came quietly.

A cargo vessel carrying lithium carbonate from Argentina to Japan reported:

GPS interference

unexplained radar echoes

a drone sighting with no transponder

a temporary blackout of satellite communications

No nation claimed responsibility.

No evidence pointed to a culprit.

But the message was unmistakable:

"Your supply chains are vulnerable."

The alliance responded with calm precision:

U.S. naval assets increased monitoring

Japan deployed maritime drones

Brazil and Uruguay coordinated coastal radar

Taiwan provided cyber-forensics

The interference stopped.

But the warning lingered.

IV. The Battle for Narrative

The opposition understood that the true battlefield was not the ocean — it was public opinion.

Media outlets in several countries began publishing:

op-eds questioning the alliance

think-tank reports predicting instability

leaked documents of dubious origin

interviews with "experts" warning of escalation

The goal was simple:

undermine trust before trust became unbreakable.

But the alliance countered with transparency:

open briefings

shared intelligence

public economic data

joint press conferences

The truth became its own shield.

V. The Silent Saboteurs

Not all opposition was foreign.

Inside Mercosur, a handful of political and business elites — long accustomed to opaque deals and foreign leverage — saw the new alliance as a threat to their influence.

They worked quietly:

delaying infrastructure approvals

leaking internal memos

stirring nationalist fears

lobbying for "neutrality"

They were not traitors.

They were relics of an older world.

A world where dependency was profitable.

VI. The Alliance Holds

Despite the pressure, the alliance did not fracture.

Japan remained steady.

Taiwan remained resolute.

The United States remained committed.

Mercosur remained united.

The opposition had underestimated something fundamental:

This alliance was not built on fear.

It was built on purpose.

And purpose is harder to break than treaties.

VII. The Shadow Retreats — But Does Not Disappear

By the end of the year, the opposition shifted tactics.

Direct interference gave way to long-term strategies:

influence networks

proxy investments

covert political funding

strategic misinformation

cyber-mapping of critical infrastructure

The shadows did not vanish.

They simply moved further from the light.

Because the rise of the Free People had changed the world —

and the world does not change without resistance.

VIII. The Lesson of the Shadows

The alliance learned a truth older than diplomacy:

Every great project creates its own opposition.

Every rising power awakens sleeping rivals.

Every new order disturbs the old.

But the shadows also revealed something deeper:The alliance was not fragile.

It was resilient.

Not because of its weapons.

Not because of its economies.

But because of its shared purpose.

And in the end, purpose is the one force shadows cannot extinguish.

"Every alliance born in the light summons an enemy born in the dark.

For power does not fear strength — it fears unity.

And the moment free nations walk together, the shadows begin to tremble."

— Cassian Delacroix, Meditations on the Unseen Forces, 1714

CHAPTER XIII — Argentina & Brazil Rebuild and Modernize Their Military Capabilities

Joint Ventures: FAdeA & Embraer — TAM 2C and KC-390 Millennium**

For decades, South America had been treated as a continent of raw materials and unrealized potential.

But alliances change destinies — and the Lithium Pact awakened something long dormant in the Southern Hemisphere:

the will to defend what they were building.

Argentina and Brazil understood that economic sovereignty meant nothing without military capability.

And so began the most ambitious defense modernization in their history — not in isolation, but in joint ventures, shared factories, and a new doctrine of hemispheric security.

I. The Awakening of the Southern Arsenal

The transformation did not begin with weapons.

It began with purpose.

Argentina sought to rebuild its aerospace industry after decades of stagnation.

Brazil aimed to consolidate its position as the region's technological leader.

Both nations realized that together they could achieve what neither could alone:

shared R&D

shared manufacturing

shared logistics

shared doctrine

The result was a binational renaissance — a rebirth of South American defense capability.

II. FAdeA & Embraer — The New Industrial Axis

Two companies became the pillars of this transformation:

FAdeA (Argentina)

Once a symbol of lost potential, now revitalized through:

Japanese investment in precision manufacturing

Taiwanese avionics partnerships

U.S. logistical support

Brazilian co-production agreements

Embraer (Brazil)

Already a global aerospace player, now expanding into:

military transport

tactical aviation

drone systems

joint training platforms

Together, FAdeA and Embraer formed the Southern Aerospace Alliance — a cooperative industrial ecosystem capable of producing world-class aircraft.

III. The TAM 2C — Argentina's Armored Rebirth

Argentina's armored forces had long been symbolic of a bygone era.

But the TAM 2C modernization program changed everything.

The upgrades included:

digital fire-control systems

thermal imaging

stabilized cannons

reinforced armor

new communication suites

Japanese-designed reliability components

The TAM 2C was no longer a relic.

It was a modern, agile, lethal platform — perfectly suited for South American terrain.

And crucially, it was built at home, with FAdeA and Brazilian suppliers providing key components.

The message was unmistakable:

Argentina would never again outsource its own defense.

IV. The KC-390 Millennium — Brazil's Gift to the Hemisphere

If the TAM 2C was Argentina's rebirth, the KC-390 Millennium was Brazil's declaration of maturity.

A multi-mission aircraft capable of:

strategic transport

aerial refueling

humanitarian relief

paratrooper deployment

medical evacuation

rapid logistics

The KC-390 became the workhorse of the new alliance, linking:

Argentine bases

Brazilian command centers

Chilean logistics hubs

Paraguayan and Uruguayan forward posts

U.S. and Japanese naval detachments

It was the aircraft that stitched the hemisphere together.

And when FAdeA began producing components for the KC-390, the partnership became irreversible.

V. The Doctrine of Southern Deterrence

Modernization was not just about equipment.

It was about philosophy.

Argentina and Brazil adopted a new doctrine:

"Defense through capability, deterrence through unity."

This doctrine emphasized:

interoperability with Japan, the U.S., and Taiwan

rapid mobility across the South Atlantic

shared maintenance and training

cyber-secure command networks

joint peacekeeping and disaster response

The Southern Hemisphere was no longer a passive observer.

It was becoming a strategic actor.

VI. The Rise of the Southern Defense Corridor

The modernization created a new industrial geography:

Córdoba: armored systems, avionics, drone labs

São José dos Campos: transport aircraft, engines, composites

Porto Alegre: electronics and cyber-defense

Mendoza: logistics and maintenance hubs

Rio Grande do Sul: naval integration

This was not just military modernization.

It was economic transformation.

Factories reopened.

Engineers returned.

Young technicians found purpose.

Supply chains grew.

Exports increased.

The alliance had created a Southern Defense Corridor — a backbone of sovereignty.

VII. The World Takes Notice

The modernization did not go unnoticed.

European analysts praised the KC-390 as a "new global competitor."

Asian strategists noted the rise of a "South Atlantic security pole."

North American observers welcomed the stability of capable partners.

Shadow opposition forces grew uneasy at the sight of a united, modernizing Mercosur.

For the first time in generations, South America was not defined by its vulnerabilities.

It was defined by its capabilities.

VIII. The Meaning of Power in the New Hemisphere

Argentina and Brazil did not seek dominance.

They sought respect.

And respect is earned through:

competence

reliability

readiness

unity

The TAM 2C and KC-390 were not symbols of aggression.

They were symbols of sovereignty.

A declaration that the Southern Hemisphere would defend its resources, its alliances, and its future.

The world had entered a new era —

and the South was no longer silent.

"A nation that rebuilds its arsenal is not preparing for war — it is preparing to decide its own fate.

And when two nations rebuild together, their enemies must learn to fear their unity more than their weapons."

— General Esteban Barcenas, Southern Defense Symposium

"Strength is not measured in steel or engines, but in the will to defend what is ours.

The KC-390 and TAM are not machines — they are the declaration that the South will never again kneel."

— Marshal Renato Alencar, Address to the Joint Aerospace Command

CHAPTER XIV — Industrial Renaissance: Naval Modernization & Drone Warfare (Paragraph Format)

Argentina and Brazil entered a new era of industrial renaissance as their shipyards, factories, and research centers roared back to life, transforming the Southern Hemisphere into a rising arsenal of maritime and aerial power. The revival began in the great shipyards of Río Santiago, Rio de Janeiro, Puerto Belgrano, and Itaguaí, where rusted cranes were restored and dry docks reopened, giving birth to modern frigates, patrol vessels, modular corvettes, and upgraded submarines designed to secure the South Atlantic's vast blue frontier. At the same time, a quiet revolution unfolded in laboratories and hangars as FAdeA and Embraer spearheaded a drone warfare renaissance, producing long-endurance surveillance UAVs, strike-capable platforms, maritime drones, electronic-warfare systems, and swarm-capable micro-drones, all linked through a cyber-secure, satellite-integrated Southern Drone Grid that made the South Atlantic one of the most monitored oceans on Earth. Brazil's submarine program expanded into a binational undersea force with Argentina, creating a stealthy shield beneath the waves, while new industrial hubs across Córdoba, São José dos Campos, Recife, Bahía Blanca, Manaus, and Rio Grande manufactured radars, engines, composites, robotics, and naval electronics, turning consumer-grade factories into sovereign defense industries. This renaissance was not an arms race but a declaration of autonomy — a doctrine of the Blue Frontier that asserted control over maritime corridors, early-warning drone networks, cyber-defense systems, and joint patrols with Japan, Taiwan, and the United States. The world watched with a mix of respect and unease as the South Atlantic transformed from a quiet ocean into a strategic theater, and Argentina and Brazil emerged not as aggressors but as capable guardians of their hemisphere, proclaiming through steel, drones, and shipyards that the South would defend what it built and shape its own future.

"A fleet is not forged from metal alone, but from the will of a people who refuse to drift.

When shipyards awaken and the seabirds take flight, the ocean learns a new truth:

the South has found its voice, and it speaks in the language of power."

— Admiral Tomás Arrieta, 1925

CHAPTER XV — Joint South Atlantic Operations: The Shield of the Free Hemisphere

The true measure of an alliance is not found in treaties or declarations, but in the synchronized movement of ships, aircraft, and minds across vast distances. After years of preparation — logistical reforms, industrial revival, naval modernization, and the rise of drone warfare — the nations of the Lithium Pact finally stepped into a new phase of their shared destiny: joint operations in the South Atlantic, the ocean that had long been treated as a quiet backwater of global strategy. Now it was becoming the proving ground of a new geopolitical geometry, one forged not by conquest but by cooperation.

The South Atlantic had always been a paradox — immense yet overlooked, rich yet underprotected, strategically vital yet strategically ignored. For decades, it was a corridor for trade, not a theater of power. But as the Lithium Pact matured, the ocean's role transformed. It became the shield of the hemisphere, the maritime frontier where the alliance would demonstrate its unity, its capability, and its resolve. The first joint operation was not a show of force; it was a show of coordination — a multinational exercise involving Argentine patrol vessels, Brazilian frigates, Japanese destroyers, Taiwanese cyber-defense teams, and American logistical support ships. Five nations, four continents, one purpose: to ensure that the South Atlantic would never again be a vacuum for foreign influence or a blind spot in global security.

The operation began with silence — the kind of silence that precedes orchestration. Satellites aligned. Drone swarms lifted from coastal bases in Rio Grande, Mar del Plata, and Montevideo. Submarines slipped beneath the waves, their lithium-powered hearts beating with the quiet confidence of modern engineering. On the surface, ships from different navies formed a single formation, their radars linked, their communications synchronized, their crews operating under a unified doctrine crafted over years of dialogue and trust. It was the first time in history that South American, East Asian, and North American forces moved as one across the southern ocean.

What made the operation remarkable was not its scale, but its philosophy. This was not an alliance built on fear or rivalry. It was built on the belief that sovereignty is strongest when shared, that oceans are safest when watched together, and that deterrence is most effective when it is cooperative rather than coercive. The South Atlantic, once a neglected expanse, became a canvas for a new kind of security — one rooted in transparency, interoperability, and mutual respect. Argentine officers learned Japanese maritime discipline. Brazilian commanders integrated Taiwanese cyber-protocols. American logisticians adapted to South American operational rhythms. Each nation contributed its strengths, and each nation learned from the others.

The drones were the first to reveal the power of this unity. Operating in coordinated swarms, they mapped the ocean with unprecedented precision, identifying anomalies, tracking vessels, and feeding real-time data into a shared command network. For the first time, the South Atlantic was not a mystery. It was a monitored, understood, and protected domain. Beneath the waves, submarines from Brazil and Japan conducted silent maneuvers, testing detection systems and communication links. On the surface, Argentine and Brazilian ships practiced coordinated patrols, while Japanese destroyers demonstrated advanced anti-submarine tactics. Overhead, long-range aircraft from the United States and Brazil conducted joint reconnaissance, weaving a web of awareness across thousands of miles.

The world watched with a mixture of curiosity and unease. Analysts in distant capitals realized that something profound had changed: the South was no longer a passive region reacting to global events. It was becoming an active shaper of its own security environment. The Lithium Pact had evolved from an economic partnership into a strategic force — not aggressive, but assertive; not expansionist, but protective; not a bloc, but a coalition of purpose. The joint operation sent a message without firing a shot: the hemisphere was no longer undefended, and its nations were no longer isolated.

Yet the most important outcome of the operation was not military. It was psychological. For the first time, the nations of the Pact saw themselves not as separate actors, but as parts of a larger whole — a hemispheric community capable of defending its resources, its trade routes, and its future. The operation forged trust in ways that no treaty could. It created habits of cooperation, shared memories, and a sense of collective identity. It transformed the South Atlantic from a geographic space into a strategic symbol — the Shield of the Free Hemisphere.

In the end, the operation was not about ships or drones or submarines. It was about the emergence of a new idea: that the South and the East, once distant and disconnected, could stand together as guardians of a shared destiny. The Lithium Pact had taken its first steps onto the world's oceans, and the waves carried its message far beyond the horizon. The shield had been raised.

"An ocean is not defended by ships alone, but by the unity of those who sail it.

When distant nations form a single horizon, even the darkest waters learn to keep their distance.

Today we did not patrol the South Atlantic — we claimed it as the shield of all who choose to stand free."

— Admiral William Brown, Address to the Fleet, Buenos Aires, 1816

CHAPTER XVI — The Breaking of the Circle: When the Confederation Meets the Empire

"Power is not proven in calm waters.

Only when the tides turn against us do we learn which alliances are built to endure."

— Aurelio Santamar, Strategist of the Southern School, 1891

Every alliance reaches a moment when its ideals collide with the world's indifference — or its hostility. For the Lithium Pact, that moment arrived not with an invasion or a declaration, but with a quiet, calculated test. A test designed to probe the Pact's unity, its resolve, and its willingness to defend the order it had begun to build. The world had watched the South Atlantic operations with a mixture of curiosity and unease. Some saw cooperation. Others saw a threat. And a few — the ones who feared a rising South — saw an opportunity to strike at the Pact's cohesion before it hardened into permanence.

The crisis began with a single vessel.

It appeared on maritime tracking systems as a research ship, flagged under a nation known for its strategic ambiguity. Its declared mission was oceanographic study. Its actual behavior told another story. It drifted into a restricted zone near a lithium-export corridor, shut off its transponder, and deployed submersible drones with signatures far too sophisticated for civilian use. The ship was not gathering data. It was gathering intelligence — mapping routes, testing response times, measuring the Pact's vigilance.

In earlier decades, such an intrusion would have gone unnoticed or unchallenged. But the South Atlantic was no longer a neglected ocean. It was the Shield of the Free Hemisphere, and the Pact's sensors — drones, radars, satellites, submarines — saw everything.

The first to detect the anomaly was a Brazilian drone swarm operating under the new Southern Integrated Grid. Within minutes, Argentine coastal radars confirmed the vessel's irregular pattern. Taiwanese cyber teams traced the drone signals to a military research institute known for its gray-zone operations. Japanese analysts identified the ship's hull modifications as consistent with intelligence-gathering platforms. The United States, monitoring from afar, quietly relayed satellite imagery showing the deployment of underwater probes.

Five nations.

Four continents.

One conclusion.

This was not an accident.

It was a probe.

The question was not what the intruder was doing.

The question was how the Pact would respond.

The decision fell to the Joint Maritime Coordination Cell — a command structure that had existed on paper for months but had never been tested in reality. Now it was being asked to act, not in simulation, but in the living ocean. The room filled with officers from different nations, speaking different languages, trained under different doctrines, yet united by a single purpose: to defend the hemisphere without escalating the crisis into conflict.

The response was measured, deliberate, and unmistakably unified.

Brazilian frigates moved first, altering course to intercept at a distance that signaled awareness without aggression. Argentine patrol vessels tightened the perimeter, ensuring the intruder had no path deeper into the corridor. Japanese destroyers, operating under a training exchange, shifted to a silent overwatch position, their sensors painting a complete picture of the vessel's capabilities. Taiwanese cyber teams launched a counter-mapping operation, feeding false telemetry to the intruder's drones. American reconnaissance aircraft orbited high above, providing a strategic umbrella.

The intruder found itself surrounded not by hostility, but by competence — a wall of coordinated presence that left no room for miscalculation.

For forty-eight hours, the standoff held. No shots were fired. No threats were issued. No speeches were made. The Pact simply existed — calm, disciplined, and immovable. And in that stillness, the intruder understood the message:

The South Atlantic was no longer a vacuum.

It was a defended space.

And the nations defending it were not alone.

Eventually, the vessel powered up its transponder, retrieved its drones, and retreated into international waters. The crisis ended as quietly as it began. But its implications echoed across the world.

For the first time, the Lithium Pact had faced a deliberate test — and passed.

The crisis revealed something deeper than capability. It revealed identity. The Pact was no longer a collection of bilateral agreements, no longer a network of trade routes and modernization programs. It had become a community of nations willing to stand together when the horizon darkened.

In capitals across the hemisphere, leaders understood the significance.

In Brasília, the defense minister remarked that unity had become "a strategic asset."

In Buenos Aires, analysts noted that the crisis had "closed the circle" of cooperation.

In Tokyo and Taipei, officials saw proof that distance was no barrier to solidarity.

In Washington, strategists recognized the emergence of a stable southern pole.

But the most profound shift occurred not in governments, but in the minds of the Pact's citizens. For the first time, they saw their nations not as isolated actors, but as part of a larger whole — a hemisphere capable of defending its resources, its trade, and its dignity.

The crisis had not broken the Pact.

It had completed it.

The circle had been tested.

And it had held.

"All alliances speak proudly in calm seas.

Only in the hour of testing do we learn which ones can hold the line.

Today the circle did not break — it tightened."

— Admiral Gian Boudin, Reflections After the Corridor Incident

CHAPTER XVII — The Dawn of Strategic Realignment

History rarely shifts in a single moment. It tilts — slowly, subtly — until the balance of the world changes without anyone realizing when the old equilibrium died. After the Corridor Incident, after the South Atlantic operations, after the circle held firm under pressure, the Lithium Pact entered a new phase of existence. It was no longer a rising alliance. It was a strategic reality, and the world began to adjust around it.

The first signs came not from the South, but from the great capitals of the North. In Washington, analysts quietly rewrote their hemispheric assessments. In Brussels, trade commissioners whispered about "the Southern Factor." In Beijing, strategists studied the Pact's logistics with a mixture of curiosity and unease. In Moscow, diplomats noted that a new axis was forming — one not aligned with any traditional bloc, yet powerful enough to influence all of them.

The Lithium Pact had become something rare in international affairs:

a coalition that others had to account for.

Its strength did not lie in military might alone, nor in economic weight, nor in technological innovation. It lay in the fusion of all three — a fusion made possible by trust, by shared purpose, and by the simple, radical idea that distant nations could build a future together without domination or dependency.

The world had grown accustomed to alliances built on fear.

The Lithium Pact was built on choice.

And that made it unpredictable — and powerful.

The first major shift occurred in the Indo-Pacific. Japan and Taiwan, emboldened by the Pact's unity, began to recalibrate their diplomatic posture. They no longer approached South America as a distant supplier, but as a strategic partner whose stability and prosperity were intertwined with their own. Joint research centers opened in Osaka, Córdoba, and Kaohsiung. Exchange programs multiplied. Semiconductor firms invested in Chilean lithium processing. Argentine engineers trained in Japanese shipyards. Brazilian cyber teams worked alongside Taiwanese specialists in Taipei's underground command centers.

The Pacific was no longer a barrier.

It was a bridge.

The second shift came from within Mercosur itself. Nations that had long viewed each other with suspicion — Argentina and Brazil, Paraguay and Uruguay, even Chile from outside the bloc — began to see themselves not as competitors, but as components of a larger strategic architecture. The Pact had given them something they had lacked for generations: a shared horizon.

For the first time, South America was not reacting to global events.

It was shaping them.

The third shift came from the markets. Investors who once dismissed the region as unstable began to reconsider. The Pact's logistics reforms, industrial renaissance, and naval modernization created a perception of reliability — a rare commodity in a world of fractured supply chains and geopolitical uncertainty. Capital flowed into ports, shipyards, battery factories, and drone labs. The South Atlantic, once a quiet corridor, became a hub of maritime commerce protected by a multinational shield.

But the most profound shift was philosophical.

For decades, the nations of the South had been told — implicitly or explicitly — that their role in the world was to supply, not to strategize; to export, not to influence; to adapt, not to lead. The Lithium Pact shattered that narrative. It proved that sovereignty was not a relic of the past, but a blueprint for the future. It showed that alliances could be built on reciprocity rather than hierarchy, on respect rather than coercion.

It demonstrated that the South could rise — not by imitating the great powers, but by becoming something new.

And yet, beneath the triumph, a quiet tension lingered. The world was changing, and not everyone welcomed the emergence of a new strategic pole. Some saw opportunity. Others saw threat. A few saw a challenge to their own influence. The Pact had passed its first test, but greater tests loomed on the horizon — tests not of ships or drones, but of diplomacy, resilience, and unity.

For alliances are not broken by crises.

They are broken by complacency.

And the Lithium Pact, now standing at the dawn of strategic realignment, faced a choice that would define its future:

Would it remain a coalition of necessity?

Or would it become a community of destiny?

The answer would shape the century.

CHAPTER XVIII — The Industrial Constellation: Toyota, Hitachi, and Toshiba in the New South

Great powers do not expand through armies alone.

Sometimes they expand through factories, through laboratories, through the quiet hum of machines that reshape continents more profoundly than any fleet. After the Lithium Pact solidified its strategic foundations, the next wave of transformation arrived not from admirals or ministers, but from three titans of Japanese industry — Toyota, Hitachi, and Toshiba. Their decision to expand operations in South America marked the moment when the Pact ceased to be merely a geopolitical alignment and became an industrial constellation, binding the hemispheres through steel, silicon, and shared ambition.

The announcement came quietly, as such world-shifting events often do. A press release in Tokyo. A ministerial briefing in Brasília. A late-night session in Buenos Aires where advisors stared at maps of industrial corridors with a mixture of disbelief and exhilaration. But beneath the formalities, everyone understood the truth: this was not investment. This was integration.

Toyota moved first.

For decades, the company had been a symbol of precision, discipline, and reliability — virtues that resonated deeply with the new South American renaissance. Its engineers saw in Argentina and Brazil not merely markets, but frontiers. The lithium triangle offered the raw materials for next-generation batteries. The revitalized shipyards and logistics corridors offered the infrastructure for global distribution. And the Pact's stability offered something rarer than minerals: predictability.

Toyota announced the creation of a tri-national production network — battery plants in northern Argentina, electric-vehicle assembly lines in Brazil, and research centers in Chile dedicated to solid-state energy systems. For the first time, South America was not exporting lithium as dust. It was exporting vehicles powered by its own minerals, refined through Japanese mastery and assembled by South American hands.

Hitachi followed with the precision of a strategist.

Where Toyota brought mobility, Hitachi brought infrastructure — the invisible skeleton of modern civilization. Its expansion focused on three pillars:

energy grids, rail systems, and industrial automation.

In Brazil, Hitachi partnered with local firms to modernize the national grid, integrating renewable energy with Japanese control systems. In Argentina, it launched a high-speed rail initiative linking Rosario, Córdoba, and Buenos Aires — a corridor that would become the economic spine of the new South. In Chile, Hitachi established robotics labs designed to automate lithium extraction with minimal environmental impact.

Hitachi did not merely build machines.

It built continuity — the kind of infrastructure that outlives governments and reshapes nations.

Then came Toshiba — the quiet architect of the digital age.

Toshiba's expansion was not measured in factories or rail lines, but in data, semiconductors, and energy storage. It established microchip packaging facilities in Uruguay, quantum-research partnerships in São Paulo, and grid-scale battery installations across the Southern Cone. Its engineers worked alongside Taiwanese specialists, creating a technological bridge between the Indo-Pacific and South America that bypassed traditional chokepoints and vulnerabilities.

With Toshiba's arrival, the Pact gained something it had never possessed before:

technological sovereignty.

Together, Toyota, Hitachi, and Toshiba formed a triad — a constellation of industrial power that transformed the Pact from a strategic alliance into an economic engine. Their presence signaled to the world that South America was no longer a supplier of raw materials, but a co-author of the technologies that would define the century.

The impact was immediate.

Ports expanded.

Railways modernized.

Factories multiplied.

Universities reformed their curricula to match the new industrial reality.

Entire cities — once stagnant — awakened with the energy of opportunity.

But the deeper transformation was cultural.

South America, long accustomed to being treated as a periphery, began to see itself as a center — a place where global giants came not to extract, but to collaborate; not to dominate, but to integrate. The Pact's philosophy of fair trade and mutual respect found its most tangible expression in these industrial partnerships.

And yet, as always, the world watched with mixed emotions.

Some saw progress.

Others saw competition.

A few saw a threat to the old order.

But none could deny the truth:

The Lithium Pact had entered a new era — one defined not by ships or drones, but by factories, research labs, and the quiet revolution of shared industry.

Toyota brought motion.

Hitachi brought structure.

Toshiba brought intelligence.

Together, they brought the future.

And South America, for the first time in its modern history, was not merely participating in that future.

It was helping to build it.

"When great nations build together, steel becomes more than metal — it becomes a covenant.

Factories rise, borders fade, and the future bends toward those who dare to shape it with their own hands."

— Kenji Takahara, Letters on the Machinery of Progress, 1874

CHAPTER XIX — A Message of Prosperity and Awareness to the World

There are moments in history when a rising power must step forward and speak — not to boast, not to intimidate, but to clarify its place in the world. After the Lithium Pact solidified its industrial foundations, after the South Atlantic became a shield rather than a vulnerability, after Toyota, Hitachi, and Toshiba anchored themselves in the Southern Hemisphere, the alliance reached such a moment. The world had begun to feel the shift — the quiet but undeniable tilt of global gravity toward the South. And so the Pact prepared a message, not of dominance, but of prosperity and awareness.

The message began in the great halls of Buenos Aires, where diplomats gathered beneath chandeliers that had witnessed centuries of ambition and disappointment. It echoed through Brasília's modernist corridors, where advisors traced new trade routes across glowing digital maps. It resonated in Santiago, Montevideo, Asunción, Tokyo, Taipei, and Washington. The Lithium Pact had matured. It had endured its first tests. It had built its first industries. And now it possessed something the world could no longer ignore:

a coherent vision of the future.

The message was crafted with precision — elegant, firm, and unmistakably sovereign:

Prosperity for those who walk with us.

Respect for those who acknowledge us.

Awareness for those who underestimate us.

It was not a threat.

It was a statement of reality.

For generations, South America had been treated as a reservoir — a place where the world extracted minerals, food, and labor, but rarely offered partnership. The Lithium Pact shattered that paradigm. It declared that the South would no longer be the world's silent supplier. It would be a co-author of the century ahead, shaping the technologies, industries, and alliances that would define the global order.

The first pillar of the message was prosperity.

The Pact opened its ports, its factories, its research centers, and its logistics corridors to nations willing to engage with respect. It offered fair trade, shared technology, and industrial integration. It invited the world to participate in a new model of development — one based on reciprocity rather than extraction, on partnership rather than dependency.

Nations that approached with sincerity found opportunity.

Nations that approached with arrogance found the doors politely closed.

The second pillar was awareness.

Awareness that the South was no longer fragmented.

Awareness that its oceans were no longer undefended.

Awareness that its resources were no longer for sale without conditions.

Awareness that its alliances were no longer optional.

This was not a warning of conflict.

It was a reminder of sovereign equilibrium.

The Lithium Pact did not seek confrontation.

But it would not tolerate exploitation.

It did not seek to dominate.

But it would not be dominated.

It did not seek to reshape the world through force.

But it would reshape the world through presence, industry, and unity.

The message spread quickly.

In Europe, analysts debated whether the Pact represented a new pole of global power.

In Asia, strategists recalibrated their assumptions about supply chains and alliances.

In North America, policymakers recognized that the hemisphere had become a partner rather than a dependent.

In rival capitals, the message was received with a mixture of caution and respect.

But the most important audience was not foreign governments.

It was the people of the South.

For the first time in generations, they saw their nations speaking with one voice — a voice that did not beg, did not apologize, did not defer. A voice that offered prosperity to the world, but demanded awareness in return. A voice that understood that peace is strongest when backed by capability, and prosperity is most enduring when defended by unity.

The Lithium Pact had become more than an alliance.

It had become a civilizational statement.

A declaration that the South would no longer be written into the margins of history.

A promise that its resources would serve its own people first.

A reminder that its sovereignty was no longer negotiable.

A vision of a world where prosperity was shared, not extracted.

The message was clear:

We rise in peace.

We prosper in unity.

We stand with awareness.

And we expect the world to do the same.

The world listened.

And the century shifted.

"Prosperity is the gift we offer the world; awareness is the respect we expect in return.

Let every nation understand this: the South rises not to replace empires, but to ensure no empire rises again."

Lorenzo di Bartolomeo Sforza, 1492

EPILOGUE — The Horizon That Remains

History does not end.

It widens.

Long after the first radars hummed over the Atlantic, long after the factories of the new South lit their furnaces, long after the Pact spoke its message of prosperity and awareness to the world, a quiet truth settled across the hemisphere: the Lithium Pact had become more than an alliance. It had become a direction — a compass pointing toward a future no longer dictated by distant capitals or inherited hierarchies.

The world had listened.

Some with hope.

Some with caution.

Some with the quiet fear reserved for forces they can no longer control.

But the Pact did not rise to threaten.

It rose to balance.

In the deserts of the Atacama, lithium brine shimmered beneath the sun like a mirror reflecting the century ahead. In the shipyards of Kobe and Rio Grande, steel bent into shapes that would patrol oceans once ignored. In the laboratories of Taipei and São Paulo, engineers whispered to machines that would define the next age of energy and intelligence. In the ports of Buenos Aires and Yokohama, containers moved with the rhythm of a world learning to breathe in unison.

And across the South Atlantic — the ocean that had once been a frontier of silence — a new constellation of nations stood watch, not as conquerors, but as custodians of a shared destiny.

The Pact had proven something rare:

that prosperity could be built without subjugation,

that alliances could be forged without fear,

that sovereignty could be defended without isolation.

But the greatest lesson was simpler still:

The South had never lacked power.

It had only lacked unity.

Now, unity had arrived — not as a sudden flame, but as a slow, steady dawn.

The world would adjust.

Some would resist.

Others would join.

All would feel the shift.

For the Lithium Pact was not merely a geopolitical arrangement.

It was a declaration that the age of passive continents had ended.

That the resources of the earth would no longer be traded without dignity.

That the oceans of the South would no longer be crossed without respect.

That the future would be shaped not by the loudest voices, but by the most steadfast.

And so the story closes not with triumph, nor with warning, but with a horizon — wide, bright, and unclaimed.

A horizon that belongs to those who dare to build.

To those who dare to stand.

To those who dare to rise together.

The Lithium Pact began as a whisper.

It became a tide.

And now, it is a world.

The rest is unwritten.

And the century is watching.

Special Thanks

To my wife, Eloise — for her unconditional support, her patience, and her unwavering belief in my vision. This work stands because you stood with me.

Books by Milton Rothbard
Geopolitical & Historical Thrillers

•The Antarctic Covenant
•The Energy Reckoning
•The Geography of Power
•The Lithium Pact
•The Lithium Triangle
•The Pact of Steel & Salt
•Pacts of Survival
•Quantum Archipelago
•The Arctic Vortex
•The Hormuz Economy

Espionage & Political Noir

•Café Buenos Aires
•The Maestro of Minds
•The Severian Manuscript
•The Parallel Shadow
•The Last Luthier
•Agent Harrison
•Project Copenhagen

Women's Romance

•The Velvet Invitation

•Giovanna's Poetry
•Curves Beneath Portofino
•Romance & Steel in Andalucia
•The Bookshop on Rue The Rivoli

Historical & Mythic Fiction

•Aurelia of Rome
•Bushido Masters
•The Andalusian Courtship
•The Chronicles of the Iron Crusade
•Viri Templari
•The Untold Story of Ypres

Crime, Mystery, Drama & Suspense

•The Watchmaker of Geneva
•The Vicarious
•My Girl of Bensonhurst (Blood in the Rain / Clan Wars)
•The Concierge

Comedy General & Corporate Comedy

•The Fool's Menu
•The Last Honest Economist
•Les Imbeciles

www.ingramcontent.com/pod-product-compliance
Lightning Source LLC
LaVergne TN
LVHW022230200926
848481LV00006B/2209
9798996279159